# MONODY OF ST. EUSTHATHIUS OF THESSALONICA

Michael Choniates

*Archbishop of Athens*

**Translated by:** D.P. Curtin

# MONODY OF ST. EUSTHATHIUS OF THESSALONICA

Copyright @ 2020 Dalcassian Press

All rights reserved. No part of this publication may be reproduced, distributed, or transmitted in any form or by any means, including photocopying, recording, or other electronic or mechanical methods, without the prior written permission of the publisher, except in the case of brief quotations embodied in critical reviews and certain other non-commercial uses permitted by copyright law. For permission request, write to Dalcassian Press at dalcassianpublishing at gmail.com

ISBN: 979-8-3302-6034-8 (Paperback)

Library of Congress Control Number:
Author: Curtin, D.P. (1985-)

Printed by Ingram Content Group, 1 Ingram Blvd, La Vergne, Tennessee

First printing edition 2020.

# MONODY OF ST. EUSTHATHIUS, *BISHOP OF THESSALONICA*

Oh, what a cursed century! Oh, our unhappy selves! How shall we bewail the magnitude of this disaster? From where shall I take words expressive enough of sorrow? For a long time I have expressed my grief, with only silent tears shed. The news of Eustathius' death struck my mind like thunder, like unexpected lightning, and I emit nothing but smoke, the sign of the innermost pain with which I am tormented. At first, I neither could nor wanted to believe the news, but for a long time I had incredulously accepted that Eustathius, like a most brilliant star fallen from the sky, had been buried in the tomb.

Amid tears and groans, my voice choked, I was not able to compose myself when I learned the painful truth. And even though I mourn the open calamity no less; now, my tears also block my voice. However, when pain does not hinder my voice, I will find some consolation, and I will fulfill the duty owed to my deceased friend. But how will I better manifest my grief by doing something? Should I fall silent like those yesterday who, as the story goes, were transformed into trees or rocks due to excessive sorrow; or should I wail and moan like those who, according to the Prophet, lament like dragons and struggle like ostriches? Both seem to me to be fitting because of the magnitude of the calamity.

O common misfortune! The loss is universal! One star of life remained, the only one of its kind. The one luminary of the world, the one sun of the sacred order. But the matter has not even been heard of: this too has been extinguished, has deserted us forever. How, o sun, have you endured not seeing the earthly sun anymore, which among mortals was what you were among the stars? But now a black fog is hovering over the whole world, darkness and night pursue the lightless life; we wander as the Egyptians once desired their shepherd taken from them, who excelled in shepherdly wisdom among all, as a shepherd among sheep; we, friends of philosophy, mourn the king of sciences, the parent of eloquence. For rightly Eustathius could boast of a royal name more than that Attic sophist; even the sacred synod seeks its eye and that voice which far and wide pronounced words worthy of a king.

# MONODY OF ST. EUSTHATHIUS OF THESSALONICA

The city of Thessalonica, yesterday very happy, today very unfortunate, because deprived of such a son as well as with grief for her spouse, a good shepherd, a wise teacher, a savior, a guardian spirit, a defender, in a word a pillar, so to speak, immovable, and if anything else praiseworthy and beneficial can be thought of, how much, I say, she longs for it with tears! Thus, consumed with grief as if she had been captured and destroyed for the second time, she lies on the ground and fears experiencing worse. For before, when the Italians were rushing in by land and sea and destroying the walls, she was snatched from the hands of the enemies by our Eustathius, whose reputation for virtues so stirred up the enemies themselves that they did not dare to look at his face, indeed the fierce army voluntarily prostrated itself at his feet. But now, deprived of this great bulwark, she lies miserably on the ground, as if captured by force and defended by no walls anymore.

What, then, does the queen of cities do in this crisis? Will she bear the misfortune more easily or more painfully, to whom Eustathius, having received benefits from him, restrained generously and returned with tokens of a grateful heart? For, whatever treasures of wisdom he generously bestowed on those who loved the noble arts while he lived there; for he was the chief of eloquence, the universal focus of wisdom, a garden open to all, a fertile field under divine auspices, a perennial source of eloquence. Hence it came to pass that disciples could reap for free and draw for free, and thirst no more for the discipline of arts and letters. For in a short time, without preludes, without prolegomena, without contests or previous studies, philosophy felt itself imbued in whoever approached him, as if he had come out of Aristotle's own school. For although he languished in deep ignorance, he first offered spiritual food. The disciple departed as if inspired by the Muses themselves. But the fruits of this tree of wisdom were not bitter like laurel leaves; rather, sweeter as a letter than Ezechiel expressed through a dream. For his honeyed tongue dripped with nectar, and rivers were saturated; therefore, his teachings penetrated deep into the soul and could not be uprooted by any force. Indeed, it seemed that the minds of all whom his teachings and discipline had filled were imbued with Chaldean potions, so to speak. You, Castle of Graces, taught your students with delightful skills, and with your voice surpassing that of the Sirens, you led them to believe what had previously been considered mythical as true. This led you to share many things with many others through the most successful method of instruction. For, instead of merely reading a book with others and explaining what needed interpretation, you elucidated difficult passages by spontaneously adding many other things that seemed relevant.

But, dear friends, I cannot recount this with dry eyes, and I always fall back into my former sorrow. For I remember with what kindness I myself, who was among his disciples, was received by him, that I might drain the cup full of wisdom. Alas! The heart is occupied by the remembrance of past times and mixes tears with blood. But stop crying, I say to myself, so that we may not only mourn the deceased man, but also fulfill the duty of admiration for his illustrious virtues. For the memory of the righteous is to be honored with modest praise, simple and properly limited. Music, according to the Wise, is an unwelcome narrative in mourning.

We have already said that it is against the norm to be initiated into both great and small mysteries at the same time; for it is a proverb that it is foolish to want to learn the art of pottery in a precious vessel. Under his auspices, however, he who as a priest initiated into the mysteries of wisdom and taught rhetoric, the disciples of the Muses entered the entrance, they beheld the most sacred place of the palace; for no province of the mysteries was closed to the neophytes. What? If any of the disciples wanted to learn the rhythm and harmony of versification or the etymology of words, they had Eustathius as a skilled guide in teaching the traditions of antiquity, and in a short time they obtained the desired solution to the problems. For he favored the studies of young people in order to open the doors to the knowledge of hidden things for the multitude. How many returned not filled with milk, but with stronger food and maturity of intellect, but let us remember greater things. Many indeed thought themselves raised to the pinnacle of eloquence and suitable for teaching others what they believed they knew, until under the auspices of Eustathius they realized how much they did not know. Many believed themselves initiated into the mysteries of the Graces, until they, being advised by him, recognized their error. More seemed to have made great progress in philosophy, until they compared themselves with that most skilled man in arts and letters. Therefore, after they had realized they knew nothing, they were not ashamed to return to the very basics and, being more advanced in age in the school of the best teacher, learn better things better. Indeed, by observing the crowds of students frequenting his home at all hours, I remember Homer speaking of bees, whose likeness countless people of all ages gathered daily to hear from him, who could not only give the standard and rules of virtue in words, but also by his own example.

Oh, how much more to be admired was his countenance, his stature than Pericles, than Xenocrates, who revealed the integrity of character at first glance! Oh, his sharp and charming conversations, equally distant from jokes and trifles as from the severity and harshness of words, indeed imbued with divine wit, as the Apostle prescribes! Truly, it was a pleasure to listen to him all day, to learn from him, and to forget his own country, as if among the Lotus-eaters. What sharpness of mind, what prudence in all things, what steadfastness of spirit in adversity, what vigor in action! What a source of virtue and wisdom was extinguished in the death of one whose memory and longing fill everyone's eyes with tears! Who will give me the tongue, who will give me the virtue of Eustathius so that I may praise him according to his worth? Without these, my praise seems to me to be a disgrace.

Eustathius shone brightly as an example of a most virtuous life and with the highest eloquence among all; for he was great in both aspects; compared to him, we are mere shadows. Who else besides him shone with equal light as a leader in philosophy and theology? Just as God once showed the way to the Israelites by day in a pillar of cloud, and by night in a pillar of fire, Eustathius fulfilled his duties with a fiery eloquence as an orator, and as a guide on the path of virtue, indeed, from here he was a resounding orator and from there a pure and eloquent priest who, like a lighthouse, showed the way to all those who were lost: for whenever words needed to be spoken due to the seriousness of the situation, with what power he moved the minds of the listeners, he even convinced his adversaries themselves, so that the whole of antiquity scarcely offers a similar example of an orator. When he was celebrating the illustrious deeds of kings, or the glory of famous patriarchs, students of all kinds were drawn to him as if by the Orphic lyre, converging from all sides to him, whose thunder and lightning resided more on his lips than in Pericles himself, who surpassed the power of Demosthenes and the vehemence of Polemon equally; who was able to give novelty to the old; who embellished whatever he said by preserving its beauty in some new way and color due to the abundance of his particular talent, equally averse to

# MONODY OF ST. EUSTHATHIUS OF THESSALONICA

ostentation and harshness, vices which are peculiar to those who, unable to reach the true sublimity of speech, descend to bombast, and, loosening the reins, fastidious with all those empty chariots, they rattle like those of Homer. For just as they make the charming beauty of his speech madly in love, yet his particular love no more than Ixion touched Juno or the suitors Penelope; nor do they see themselves deceived by any image or seductive arts. There were also those who, like beginners, used unusual words and tropes, yet they did not succeed in what they attempted, neither in poetry nor in prose, where they were accustomed to put a purple cloth on cheap bodies, nor did they succeed in rhetoric. For in this, they did not impose a foreign garment on the cheap form (as it is said that Alexander put a Persian garment over his Macedonian cloak), until Eustathius boldly emerged as the protector of the art of oratory, which was then especially in him, in order to be erased from the chorus of arts, which until then had been teaching the principles of art and exhorting to the imitation of the ancient models those who had imprudently neglected the rules of rhetoric, in a short time to a new. He restored the cultivation of that art of his which was dearer to our ancestors than anything else. So, when his disciples compared their own declamations with those of Eustathius, they could not help but see a vast difference, like that of still water from the Pactolus flowing down from the heights of Mount Lebanon with a pleasant murmur, as if we were speaking with Solomon; so whoever considers the eloquence of our author to be sophistical, unjust critics they will be to me. For just as the Macedonians believed that Alexander had been transformed into Pyrrhus the Epirote due to his swiftness in battle and his harsh character; so from Eustathius the image of a distinguished orator was placed before the eyes of the audience; indeed, one single figure of Eustathius, which represented something most excellent and a model of oratorical elegance, surpassed all others, as if an artist, from many exceptional women, had taken what was most outstanding from each and had created a painting complete in every detail.

Just as someone who would judge the beauty of a painting as being located in only one part of it would make a wrong judgment in the art of painting; so too in this case, someone who compares an excellent orator to one of the great ancient orators solely for the sake of one virtue would judge very wrongly about the man himself, not admiring enough even if he measured the whole sun from just one ray. However, someone would judge our author better who, by imitating a poet who attributes the eyes of Jove, the stature of Mars, and the chest of Neptune to Agamemnon, would compare him to the man we are now praising, then to another for another virtue, and finally to a third for a third virtue, and for the sake of that one thing for which he was thought to be perfect, you will have discovered the ultimate perfection of Eustathius' oratory.

Let us now briefly outline his eloquence in words. With what abundance of ideas, with what joy in creating, how melodious his voice, how manly his delivery, how well-arranged his features! What appropriateness of words in suitable places! What roundness of speech! Indeed, I believe that if anything seems to be lacking in knowledge or eloquence, the listener or emulator of Eustathius' wisdom and speech will be found wanting. It will be enough for each to have grace, enough dignity where they can incorporate something of Eustathius' speech into their own, even if it may seem slight. Thus, all pursuits depended on him as if on a god of eloquence, so that whatever he uttered was in the place of divine voice and rule, and not absurdly in line with that saying of the Pythagoreans: He himself said, I think.

Therefore, it is not surprising if two parts of the earth claim such a stronghold of virtue and wisdom for themselves. For our city has already been beloved by many gods; for this reason, the contest is now called the Olive Grove and the Amphitheater of Pirmeus. The same thing has almost happened to us too. Lycia has claimed you as its leader, O excellent man, who surpasses all with the brightness of your soul; for it was fitting for you to shine as a bishop in the Church, like Christ, who was already clothed in righteousness as a priestly garment. But before you began your priestly wedding song, beloved Thessalonica, recognizing and envying your rival, pretended to be a widow to win you as a husband. Thus, a fierce contest erupted between the two Churches, and truly someone might say that Europe and Asia contended to see which one would possess you. For one of them strives for you, as someone who was once a groom, and you were hardly able to bear it if your bride was not as she had been, and moreover, if the myrrh native to the eastern sky delighted in being postponed to another. The other, the first among the cities of the West next to the imperial city, and soaked in the precious blood of martyrs, was deeply troubled by the thought of being deprived of you, a man of such importance. Therefore, she left nothing untouched, neither in word nor in deed, until she became your bride. Indeed, I am convinced that it will never happen that she will be joined to a better man; for the future will never bring forth a man like you for her. For just as once Philopoemen was the last illustrious leader of the Greeks, so in Christ, time, fertile in events and voracious in bringing things to light, has produced you as the last bishop.

For who else besides you will be born with equal dignity of character, a thunderbolt of eloquence, an orator, a holy judge, so to speak, as if from Christ's throne, rendering oracles from the top of Mount Sinai? Who will ever match you in the sanctity of life, in the power of eloquence? It was given to very few to follow the course of your thoughts, to listen to your teachings, those whom it pleased to hear the sound of the divine voice even at the foot of the mountain. Therefore, no one was not delighted in your presence, if perhaps a ravenous beast appeared, whether a lion, a tax collector devouring our entrails, or a spotted panther, that is, a domestic ruler, or a wolf, an enemy and ambusher of the flock. All these, in your presence, stood in a hidden place, so as not to be touched by your words as if by so many stones. What wonder is it then? For even kings themselves could not bear to look upon you with an unmoving countenance and equable mind, indeed, as disciples, they listened to your words and behaved modestly. The Psalms proclaim the name of God as holy, as light, indeed as devouring fire. The many-eyed Seraphim do not gaze directly at his face, but from an oblique angle with half-open eyes, and they barely spread their wings. In the same way, this visible sun will be a most delightful star only to those who are content with enjoying its rays. But whoever dares to gaze directly at it with unblinking eyes will do so not without penalty and with great harm to his sight. In the same way, no one but a completely imprudent and rash person would approach you, who make the divine sun, speaking empty or incongruous things: for whoever was reproved by you thought he suffered the same as if the earth were to split open before his feet. For in teaching the arts of the Muses, you used true knowledge and discipline, unlike that strenuous man who, being like Homer, also accused his own shortcomings. Likewise, by reason, not by force, you compelled the minds of the guilty and the accused to confess their fault and accept reproof leading to repentance. Thus, to you, most venerable man, chaste beauty was added, and the honorary incantation of sanctity followed you as a bulwark everywhere. You, who at first seemed less worthy, with the help of reason and speech, and sometimes with the purification power of water, led them to repentance. That Clearchus, a Lacedaemonian by birth, as Xenophon testifies, with a grim face and a very hoarse voice, was nevertheless not an obstacle to being a splendid and cheerful standard-bearer in battle to his soldiers. Your gentleness of character always greeted those who met you with a pleasant demeanor, and this was true even when you were inflamed with righteous anger against the wicked. Who could be reproached by you, as long as he was not base in spirit, and not be content, hearing consoling words rather than reproaches, valuing roses more than thorns? Thus, your gentleness was not without a sting, which was needed to give force to your admonitions; nor did your acrimony lack in pleasantness, for both were happily blended together. You yourself well knew that those things which you either labored over with sweat or composed in jest, were avoided by students of letters, since your affairs, repeated in the forum and public streets, had become a proverb.

So many and such good men followed by the mourning of all citizens, especially of that city which, as a wife deprived of her husband, sits overwhelmed with grief on the ground, indeed refusing all consolation and throwing herself onto the tomb of the deceased, she indulges so much in sorrow that her tears wet her cheeks, as if I were speaking with Jeremiah. For the crown had already fallen from her head, and the wife preferred to be buried rather than be deprived of her husband; indeed, if it were allowed, she was ready to sacrifice herself to her husband, like Panthea, the most loving wife of her husband according to Xenophon.

These things, however, she said with weeping and lamenting: "Who without deep groans, who without tears, has heard the message brought? Wretched me! The excellent shepherd who gave his life for me has died; the wise man who excelled in many virtues, my bishop, the great Eustathius, a venerable and famous name! Wretched me who lost my husband, to whom I was once happily married, and who has now been snatched away from me by death; who recently, to speak with David, clothed me in scarlet and luxuries." A golden ornament adorned my worship, that is, with splendid prayers. But now, when it is silent, stripped of its ornament, I walk clad in black garments and in the darkness of widowhood, with every shade of blackness. Let it not be that anyone in ancient Rome or in the other cities of Italy brings the news of Eustathius' death as a joyful message, lest the proud and envious rejoice in our calamity and attack certain articles of faith with a new ardor, which they have not dared to do until now, fearing the victorious eloquence of Eustathius. Thus the man has departed from the living, to whom the whole world was not worthy. Alas! I have lost my protection. And how can I myself not fall in desperate circumstances? Hereafter, cruel waves will assail me, deprived of my defense, which previously had been dashed against the rocks and turned into foam! The meadow that I love has been ravaged by death, the Sicilian war, which destroyed all divine and human buildings, as if leaving untouched a sacred grove for the gods. Now the precious balm of wisdom has been poured out, which attracted all lovers of excellent things with its sweet fragrance; and from both, yesterday I tasted the sweet fragrance of life according to the words of Christ through Paul; but now I am suffocated by the horrible smell of death. With that life, the graceful mouth of the deceased, the instrument of great freedom, has perished! The balmy lips have fallen silent. The fiery language has been extinguished. O most venerable archetype of wisdom, and fortress of prudence! O perpetual eyes, true indicators of joy, who truly showed delight, who demonstrated chastity, where have you gone? Be present, Philosophy, be present, Rhetoric, promoted so greatly by Eustathius! Be present also, Grammar, with your attendants: I appoint you wise mourners, according to the words of the prophet, so that, even though you are widows yourselves, you may lament greatly with me for the great bridegroom. For not only, like the patriarch Jacob, did he lead two wives of knowledge, but he was the husband of all; not the leaders of just one people in the number of ten, but he fathered the leaders of all the provinces of Rome. For this reason, I call upon all cities, bound by a common ancestor in spirit, to join me in lamentation; but above all, the ancient, new Zion, whose most excellent son (according to the words of the prophet) whom he loved uniquely, has departed. Thus, surrounded by a larger crowd of mourners, I will be present at the common calamity. For just as the Egyptians mourned Jacob for a long time with Joseph and his family, so many foreigners follow the apostolic salt of the Roman land, the universal evangelical sun that sheds its brilliance of virtue and wisdom from here and there, in their longing. For this sun did not shine only on me, but through the whole nourishing earth it sent forth its rays. But now, where the common lighthouse of all lies extinguished, not a brief, but a long-lasting, indeed eternal darkness occupies the earth, after the shining star of the sepulcher has been devoured. Through these shadows, with just predators and thieves, dear friends, what a wretched calamity awaits me! I will be a prey to tax collectors and revenue officers, and I will be more welcome than an excellent shepherd who does not protect, with individual care and concern, what he follows. For Eustathius now sleeps the eternal sleep, stripped of the weapons with which he used to defend us against the wicked; whereas another shepherd, David, was the one who killed the bear and the lion, the robber, and rescued the sheep from the glutton, just as a shepherd, as the Scripture testifies, who pulled a leg or the tip of an ear from the mouth of a lion. Either he poured out prayers to the Lord, or he moved the hearts of kings, and bad luck vanished. Now alas! After he had reclined to rest in his bed, he passed away without me being present, on his final day. How will I, a wretched survivor, be without such a great man?

This and similar things she will lament with a groan in Thessalonica when she mourns the dead and in vain will always strive for the life of a dear one, especially among adverse circumstances, she will remember. Indeed, you, most blessed and wisest bishop, departed from life with the utmost tranquility, afflicted by no disease, troubled by no earthly cares; for you shed your body like a garment without pain of soul. For you took care of the body's members in accordance with reason, so as to delay death as long as possible. Just as a globe touches only one point on the surface of the earth, so also your body touches your soul as little as possible, lest it be harmed by the pleasures of the senses. Then, when you were struggling in the sleep that releases cares, you gave rest to your eyes and times; then in the first sleep you replaced another, a long sleep interrupted by a brief one, a gentle one hard, and thus you slept the sleep of the saints of God that pleases the Lord. Immortal hands did not close your eyes, nor did your limbs, contracted with cold, lay you down on the bed; but sweet and enchanting sleep, when you were lulled and joyous in spirit, through the gates of dreams led you to death, or, more truly we say, from this earthly abode to that heavenly homeland, just as Ulysses, after various adventures, not buried in sleep on an island not his own, but reached his own where he had been born. Following the example of the patriarch Jacob, after finishing the instructions with which you instructed your sons, you placed your feet on the bed and passed away; like Jacob, you ascended the ladder.

You have seen not through sleep, but truly, at whose level you have passed through, from moderation in worldly affairs as a starting point, freeing the soul from desires, establishing a spiritual kingdom, attributing the highest degree to divinity; the ladder, by which the angels ascended and descended, showing you the way, and Eustathius, who was being prepared for contemplation through the episcopate, leading you from contemplation to the very vision of God. Thus, the ladder also reached the sky before your eyes, and at its peak God resided; through which, leaving us on the ground, you ascended to God through the midst of angels, becoming God yourself, and it seems to me that you have completed your journey like an apostle. For undoubtedly, just as Peter, the chief of the apostles, you too were held in prison with two chains, bound by sleep and body, but the angel of the Lord, as he once came to him at night, now came to you, and immediately the chains fell from your feet, freed from the bonds of the one who was leading your soul, you followed. Perhaps you also, like Peter, seemed to see a vision, and you doubted whether the things done by the angel were true, until the gate was opened spontaneously and you went out into the city, well fortified, where you truly saw that the Lord had sent his angel to deliver you from the hands of death. I believe that you found the Lord himself awakened in the middle of the night, girded with a belt of righteousness. For although your body may have been asleep, your mind was awake, like the wise virgins, adorning the burning lamp. Therefore, you were ready to meet the Bridegroom at the untimely hour of the night.

At the golden age, you truly appear to have survived, and as it happened, you died entangled in sweet sleep, indeed after death carried in a chariot of sleep and death. You were being carried through the land of the living, and joyfully through the gates of heaven opened, dressed in the archiepiscopal robe of glory, you were being kindled to perform sacred duties entrusted to you. There before you, and in your honor, those who perform sacred rites around Aaron and Samuel will rise, not only because you excel in a wonderful way among the bishops of the Church, but because your tunic, adorned with more golden bells than theirs, was interwoven with scarlet pomegranates; therefore, as a preacher of the Gospel and as an orator of the law, you surpassed them by shining with obscure symbols. There you will have encounters with men adorned with the most gifted talents of mind and soul, Clement and Dionysius, rejoicing in you as a brother - who, following their example, subjected Greek philosophy to Christian philosophy, a diligent servant of the holy lady at home. You are received as a most welcome guest by Basil and Gregory, and they judge you worthy to cohere with those who, like you, excel in prayers.

They adorned the Church with jewels more precious than silver or gold. The Phineas also lead the college to their side without hatred and envy; for they know well that you have rebuked those who have fallen into impiety with sharper words than a sword. Finally, Christ, the living word, the wisdom of all creation, places you on his right near the throne, offering you a cup greater than wisdom, presenting you with a new potion to drink with the perfect people in the paternal kingdom, destined for all time: "For Solomon says, he loves no one except the one who dwells with wisdom." But you, who constantly abide with her, were captivated by the charms of wisdom alone, indeed you lived with her as with a wife, you died with her, and now, freed from all the miseries of the body, you have attained a portion of her eternal fountain.

If you look upon us, the inhabitants of the earth, dear soul, as you truly do; for the mystical voice teaches us that this is an honorable reward for the righteous, like you, or a pledge of the promised blessings, which eye has not seen, ear has not heard, and which have never entered into the heart of man, do not reject this sacrifice of tears, which I offer to you, though not poured out over your tomb (which is not given to me for the sake of consolation); although these tears, not sufficiently seasoned with the honey of your praises. You also entrust me with a drop of your grace; for such duties to perform, if you are willing, you are now more capable than ever before. We will not see each other again with our eyes, we will not converse through letters; for there is an immense space between the earth and the starry sky, that is, between us; however, we do not despair of being together with you. This obstacle must also be overcome by us, although it will be after some time. But now another obstacle much more horrible and no less than the distance between Abraham's bosom and the abyss of hell has come to my mind, where crossing over from either side is not allowed. Indeed, you dwell among the blessed, but for us it is most feared that we may be condemned to the same punishment as the companions of that burning rich man and be separated from you for eternity; this separation deeply troubles my soul both now and in the future. May God, out of mercy and your grace, grant that we may hear Moses and the prophets and believe in the testimony of Christ the Lord who rose from the dead, and that we may repent sincerely, so that we may not be cast into that place of dreadful torments, but be considered worthy to offer sacred prayers to Almighty God with you. Let us enter with awe into the most holy sanctuary of the true tabernacle, not built by human hands, and let us approach with a pure and humble sacrifice.

The Scriptorium Project is the work of a small group of lay people of various apostolic churches who are interested in the preservation, transmission, and translation of the works of the early and medieval church. Our efforts are to make the works of the church fathers accessible to anyone who might have an interest in Christian antiquities and the theological, philosophical, and moral writings that have become the bedrock of Western Civilization.

# MONODY OF ST. EUSTHATHIUS OF THESSALONICA

To-date, our releases have pulled from the Greek, Syriac, Georgian, Latin, Celtic, Ethiopian, and Coptic traditions of Christianity, and have been pulled from sundry local traditions and languages.

www.ingramcontent.com/pod-product-compliance
Lightning Source LLC
LaVergne TN
LVHW061044070526
838201LV00073B/5182